This book is dedicated to my Uncle Gerry.
May his spirit and poetry be a guide for the world. As he wrote,
"What a better world this would be
if we lived side by side peacefully."
To my family and friends for their faith in me,
and reminding me that I am never alone.

A Few Words About This Story...

"Wunce upon a time in the land of Wuu, there lived a young girl named Wanda-Luu." These words came to me while I was on a mountaintop, alone, surrounded by beauty and no other sound but the whistling wind. The story was completed when I returned from my solo wilderness trip in about 45 minutes, very much as you will see it here.

After telling the story to hundreds of people at schools, camps, and story-circles, I am delighted to finally share it in picture book form! **The Adventures of Wanda-Luu** is a story about discovering self awareness, the process of getting to know the "two yous" inside: the actor and the witness, the listener and the speaker, the questioner and the answerer.

The Adventures of Wanda-Luu is for all ages. Read it out loud to a younger person, making up different voices for the different characters, and ask each other questions after each chapter (there are questions to raise at the end of the book). Or just read it yourself, tucked under the covers. I invite you to write your own story using Wanda-Luu's story writing guide.

I hope that you always double your fun in all your adventures!

With Warm Wonderful Wishes ~
Dr. Wendy

The Adventures of Wanda-Luu

A W-FUN! STORY

Chapter One: What, No Fun?

"Wunce" upon a time in the land of Wuu,
there lived a young girl named Wanda-Luu.

Wuu was a land with a valley below and
many a hill where the winds would blow.

But in Wuu, Wanda-Luu was lonely
and sad,
because she was alone—
well, except for Daddy-O, her dad.

Daddy-O, it seemed, knew just what to do—
not only for himself, but also for Wanda-Luu.
He often would yell whenever she'd sing,
or play her whistle, or do any fun thing!

CLEAN UP, WANDA-LUU!!!
Don't sit and play!!!
There's more work to do, so put the flute away!
You can't have fun and clean these floors well!
No playing in Wuu— it's as clear as a bell!!!

But Wanda-Luu thought that this was wrong—
to be yelled at for simply singing a song!
She tried to tell him, but Daddy-O wouldn't listen,
and then she would cry until her cheeks glistened.

One day, after Wanda had scrubbed ALL the floors,
she took a short break from ALL of the chores.
She got so sad, she began to cry,
and one big tear rolled out of her eye.

Welcome to Wuu

And like that tear, she wanted to roll,
down her own path, to find her own goal.
And right then she decided to go— Oh No!

Before she left,
she scribbled a note:

"I am leaving, Daddy-O..."

was not all she wrote.

P.S. "I hope you'll understand.
I want to be ALL that I can.
So goodbye for a while,
I will return soon,
but for now, I must leave,
while there's light from the moon."

And then she signed it:

"Love, Wanda-Luu"

And late that night,
she left the land of Wuu—
with some water,
her whistle,
and a cookie or two.

When Daddy-O awoke, he gave a big yawn.
(He always did this at the break of dawn).

But instead, he found her note
under his door.
He picked it up slowly
and read with dismay—

was all he could say,
and two tender tears
rolled down his fat cheeks—
('twas the first time he cried
in twelve hundred weeks!)

All through the day, he tried to work with the sheep,
and he cried as he cooked for his sadness was deep.
He could barely lift a mop, he was so sad and blue.
He longed to hear the voice of playful Wanda-Luu!

That night, through his tears, he wished on a star,
that Wanda-Luu would be safe and would come to no harm.
He re-read her note two hundred times more,
saying…

Chapter Two: Where Are You?

Deep into the woods Wanda wandered alone.
She walked and she walked far away from her home.
"It sure is quiet in these woods," she declared.
For the very first time, Wanda-Luu felt scared.

W-w-where am I?

she asked out loud to a tree.

Where you are
(said a voice)
is listening to me!
And isn't this
just WHERE you
wanted to be?

"WHAT was THAT!?!?!" screamed Wanda-Luu with a shriek.
"I didn't know that a tree could speak!?!"

Why, that's true!

(said the Voice
that was quite clearly heard)

You spoke in your mind Wanda—every single word!!!
You simply asked a question, and you yourself replied.
You needed an answer and a friend to get by.
Just ask yourself a question and you'll soon know what to do,
for I am your best friend and guess what? I'm YOU!!
So, Where shall you go,
Miss Wanda-Luu?

So Wanda-Luu asked herself,

Where shall I go?
To the west or the south
where the warmer winds blow?
Where do I like best?
The mountains or the city?

She thought of the places
she heard were quite pretty.

She remembered the places she had been to before
and imagined the future
and then thought some more.
She thought of Wuu, and the valley,
and even outer space.
Yes, Wanda imagined every sort of place!!!

"Gosh! This is easy!" she sang out with glee
"I can be any place when I *choose* WHERE to be!"
Wanda-Luu was so happy she skipped until night
and she played on her whistle and forgot all her fright!

"WHO," asked an Owl, "is this strange looking bear,
who dances around with her snout in the air
and yells this silly *'WOW'* without any care?"

"Well, it's me, Wanda-Luu. I hope you're not mad.
If I woke you, I'm sorry, it's just that I'm glad!"

"Who you are," squawked the Owl, "is not just your name,
unless you are in some Wanda-Luu Hall of Fame.
I never heard of a 'Wanda-Luu',
so tell me, small loud one, just who, who are you?"

Wanda tried to explain why she shouted with glee.

"Well, tonight I just learned that I choose where to be,
by asking *me* a question that was answered by *me!*"

"Just who is this '*me*' that you choose to speak of?
Who are you, Wanda-Luu? Speak up, me love!"

"I'm a singer, and a writer, I can whistle and swim,
when I cook, I'm a chef," is what she told him.

But, then slowly Wanda-Luu hung her head in shame.

"But I'm also a bad daughter with no one to blame.
See, I didn't like what my dad had to say,
so I guess I decided to go away.
I just didn't know what else I could do,
and so now I'm alone trying to talk with you.
I did what I could, but I'm not very old—"

"WANDA-LUU!!!"
screeched the Owl,
"These all sound like roles!
Are you really what you're doing
or what you have done?
Wanda-Luu,
I believe that you are NO ONE!!!"

And just then, the Owl swooped down on her head.
He flew round and round and her face got beet red.
Wanda-Luu tried to fight him by punching
the air, but with his large wings,
he tangled her hair!

"STOP FLYING!!!"

screamed Wanda to the Owl (who knew).

"I am not no one! In fact, I AM TWO!!!
I AM TWO when I watch while I work at a task!
I am two, one that answers AND one that can ask!!!
I am listening AND talking at the very same time
AND I AM WHO I AM when I make up this rhyme!!!"

Well, the Owl stopped flying around and around,
and he settled himself on a branch that he found.

"Who you are is quite clear in this song that you yell!
You're a smart Wanda-Luu, it's as clear as a bell!
I must now confess that I tried to get you mad,
so you'd see that who you are is not all that bad!
In fact, who you are is quite brilliant, you see,
I didn't know I was two, 'til I turned twenty-three!
So keep asking questions and I'm sure you'll go far
and I'm sure you'll keep finding **you are who you are**!
And maybe someday you will ask yourself, 'Why?' "

And then, he flew off—
Without saying good bye!!!

Chapter Four: Wuu Is Different Than Before.

So, Wanda-Luu, alone again, saw it was dawn
and she had many questions since the Owl had gone.
She thought of Daddy-O, who was quite far away, and
wondered what was *he* feeling since she left yesterday?

The sun would soon rise, it was nearly past five,
when she jumped—

"Daddy-O doesn't know I'm alive!"

And she realized she had to get back very soon,
and if she left now she might get back by noon!

But how should I go back?
Which way shall I go?

So she wished to the Wind to help her to know.

"Will you show me the way?" Wanda-Luu asked out loud,
and the Wind began blowing a small western cloud.
She followed that cloud through the woods where it blew...

and before she knew it…

she was back in WUU!!!

Daddy-O!

She cried as she leaped down the hill.
Her father was waiting there, very, very still.
But as she ran toward him, he held out his arms,
and they hugged and they danced
right there on the farms!!!

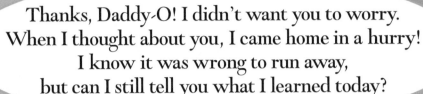

So she took out her whistle and made up a song.

By asking ourselves 'What?' and 'Where?' and 'Who?'
And questions that begin with the letter 'W'!
You can double yourself—it's W-Fun!
You see, Daddy-O, we are not just one.
With 'two yous' inside us, we're never alone
and now that I know this, I'm glad to be home!
We can learn who we are, and where we can be,
when we ask ourselves questions, we'll double you and me!

Then Daddy-O smiled and said,
"Gosh, I learned something 'two'!!!"
and he yelled a big

WOW!!!

just like Wanda-Luu!

The End

Questions About the Story

These questions are for you to think about or discuss with the person reading this to you. Both Daddy-O and Wanda-Luu learn a lot about themselves and make positive changes by the end of the story.

Chapter 1 Questions:

1. Why do you think Wanda-Luu wanted to leave Wuu? Have you ever felt this way? When and why?

2. What main emotion does Wanda-Luu feel with Daddy-O? Why?

3. What do you think she needs?

4. Have you ever felt like someone didn't understand or really listen to you? When?

5. What are some things that people do if they feel misunderstood or not listened to?

6. Why do you think Daddy-O yells at Wanda-Luu?

7. What main emotion does Daddy-O feel at first? Why? How does Daddy-O feel when he finds Wanda-Luu's note? What does he realize?

8. Do you think Daddy-O understands Wanda-Luu? Do you think Wanda-Luu understands Daddy-O? What could help them get along better?

9. What do you think about Wanda-Luu's idea to leave home? What else could she have done? What would you have done?

Chapter 2 Questions:

1. What was Wanda-Luu feeling when she first walked through the woods? Have you ever felt this way? When?

2. What are the qualities of a best friend?

3. What does it mean to be "your own best friend?" Are you "your own best friend"? What can you do to become your own best friend?

4. What is "imagination"? How can you use your imagination?

5. If you could go anywhere, using your imagination, where would you want to go? What would you like to do? Why?

6. Why was Wanda-Luu so excited? Have you ever felt this way? When?

7. What would you like to ask Wanda-Luu?

Chapter 3 Questions:

1. What did the owl ask Wanda-Luu? Why do you think he asked her this?

2. Why do you think the owl didn't like most of her answers?

3. Like Wanda-Luu, have you ever felt bad about something you did because you knew it was wrong? When?

4. Is Wanda-Luu bad because she ran away? Why?

5. Have you ever felt like Wanda-Luu did when the owl flew around? Have you ever gotten really angry at someone? Why? What did you do? When?

6. What answer did Wanda-Luu give that the owl finally liked? Why did he like it?

7. How would **you** answer the question "who are you"? Do you think the owl would like your answer?

8. How do you think Wanda-Luu felt when she realized that Daddy-O might be worried about her? What did this motivate her to do?

9. Have you ever thought about how other people may feel because of your actions or when you are away from them? When?

Chapter 4 Questions:

1. What helped Wanda-Luu get back home?

2. How did Daddy-O react to Wanda-Luu's coming back?

3 How was Daddy-O different at the end of the story? What do you think made him change?

4. How was Wanda-Luu different? What do you think made her change?

5. What can you do when you feel lonely or feel that nobody understands?

6. What can you do when you don't get along with someone, especially a parent?

7. How does it feel to be really listened to? How does it feel to really understand someone else?

8. What questions are important to ask of yourself?

9. Why is it important to know yourself?

10. Why is it important to know yourself and be "your own best friend"?

A Word About Stories

Many stories and fairy tales follow the pattern of a main character facing some challenge in life and then returning home with a new wiser, perspective. There is usually a big lesson to be learned about change and being a better person.

In "The Adventures of Wanda-Luu," Wanda- Luu learned at least 3 important things in the story:

1. You are your own best friend.

2. You get to know yourself and be a better friend to yourself by asking yourself questions and answering them.

3. Your imagination is important and can help you find creative solutions to problems.

Daddy-O learned at least 3 important things in the story:

1. All work and no play makes a person very grumpy.

2. Sometimes you don't appreciate others until they're gone.

3. You can learn a lot from listening to children.

Both Daddy-O and Wanda-Luu make positive changes by the end of the story.
I hope you will '"two"!

Before writing your own story, thing about your answers to the following questions:

1. What was one of your favorite storybooks when you were younger?

2. Why was this one of your favorites?

3. What were some of the qualities that the main character had?

4. Could you personally relate to any of these qualities? That is, were any of these qualities ones that you had or wanted to have? What were they?

5. What is a positive quality that you and the main character of this story have in common?

6. What was one of the challenges the main character faced? How did she or he face the challenge?

7. What is a hero? What would make you a hero in your own life?

Wanda-Luu's Six Simple Steps to Story Writing

Now use the following steps so that you can write your own story!

Step 1: Think about a time when you discovered something or learned an important lesson—about life or about yourself. Some important lessons are about friendship, respect, feeling good about being different, losing something or someone, moving, learning how to love and care for someone or something, learning how to say no, etc.

Story Lesson/Theme:_____

Step 2: Create a character that will learn what you have learned. It could be an animal or a person with another name that you like. Draw a picture of this character. (In W-Fun!, I used the first letter of my real name and came up with the name "Wanda-Luu and drew a cartoon of how I thought she would look")

Main Character Name_____

Step 3: Create a place for this character. Start with "Once upon a time..." Use your imagination to describe a place that your character would live. Draw a picture of this place or cut out a picture from a magazine. (In this story, Wuu looked like the place that I was camping when I first got the idea for this story.)

Place of story_____

Other characters_____

Step 4: Describe something that isn't quite right in this place and make up other characters who can either help or challenge the main character. All good stories have conflict. Perhaps it was the way the lead character was treated, or there was something wrong with them or their environment. You can make up as many other characters as you need in the story, but try to have no more than 3 or 4 total. Otherwise, it can get confusing! (In this story, there are 3 main characters. The conflict was mainly between Wanda-Luu and Daddy-O. The owl character helped Wanda-Luu to see herself more clearly, by questioning her and getting her to think hard, whether she liked it or not!)

Challenge_____

Step 5: Find a solution to the problem that exists. Conflicts want solutions. The character now has to solve this problem, until the best solution is found. (For example, Wanda-Luu's first solution was to leave Wuu—probably not the best solution. The real solution was when she learns that she is her own best friend and then comes back home to tell a very happy Daddy-O what she learned about herself in the woods.)

Solution_____

Step 6: Finally, have the character share what they've learned with another character in the story. Your main character should say something about what they have discovered, showing that they have learned something about themselves, life, and or the world. And that's the end! Share your story with a friend!

Acknowledgments

Every book has a story behind it. This book would not be in your hands without the help of so many wonderful people. I am especially grateful to: my parents who welcomed me back to New Jersey after many years away; Wendy Keilin, coach and book *doula*, for her daily phone calls urging me to complete another page; Debra Russell for leading *The Artist's Way* group and her fine coaching acumen, Ed Merritt, my 'A-Way' buddy, for help with scanning and moral support; Chris Komuves for exposing me to Jasc® Paint Shop Pro®; Wendy and Mike Running Wolf for asking me to tell the story at their celebrations, breathing new life into Wanda-Luu.

From my time in the Rocky Mountains, I thank David LaChapelle for teaching me the subtle power of solitude. Kudos to Jesse Manno for initial editing. Much gratitude to David Coddington for believing in Wanda-Luu. Thanks to my students at the University of Colorado and many folks in Boulder for their insights and their own stories after hearing about Wanda-Luu.

Pats on the back and hugs to Pat Hickey for scanning and musical accompaniment at the 2/02/02 "W-Fun!" book-launching party; Elaine Schenkel and Jill Gerken Wodnick for deep friendship; Cecilia "CC" for massages and talks; Laura Zam, Denise Woods & Olga Botcharova for the magic of 'wishcraft'; Craig Mulgrum for laser printing, Duncan Ewald, my story book teacher, for his inspiration and assistance; Jack Cuffari for promo tips, Tabitha Felix and Frannie Schram for meticulous editing; Gaby Bailey for the chance to teach her middle school students about stories. A big WOW!!! to the scholars who performed the story at the Governor's School of Public Issues, Yay! to Ricky Contreras, book designer, for the extra hours of input.

I also give a heartfelt thank you to Najeeb Alli (aka Nod, as in "Winken, Blinken and…") for his encouragement, theories, hugs, and technical assistance.

Finally, I thank YOU, dear reader, for being right here right now!

Wendy Davis has a Ph.D. in Sociocultural Psychology from the University of Colorado, Boulder. While there, she also received an honorary degree in 'W-ology' from a friendly British owl named Desmond. She has taught classes in psychology, statistics, world history, and now teaches yoga, workshops in diversity and public speaking. Wendy is currently the director of CPR Educational Consulting, Creating Positive Results by empowering students to be leaders in their schools on various issues. Along with writing and drawing, she enjoys singing, hiking, biking, playing flute and ocarina and traveling to beautiful places. This is her first book.

Printed in the United States
by Baker & Taylor Publisher Services